The Chaldean Oracles

Mystical Wisdom of the Cosmos and Divine Realms

A Modern Translation

Adapted for the Contemporary Reader

**Julian the Theurgist
(or Ancient Chaldean Magi)**

© Copyright 2025. All rights reserved.

It is not legal to reproduce, duplicate, or transmit any part of this document in either electronic means or in printed format. Recording of this publication is strictly prohibited and any storage of this document is not allowed unless with written permission from the publisher except for the use of brief quotations in a book review.

Table of Contents

Preface - Message to the Reader 1

Prologue 3

Introduction 7

The Oracles of Zoroaster 23

Ideas 30

Particular Souls 37

Matter 42

Magical And Philosophical Precepts 49

Oracles From Porphyry 59

Thank you for Reading 63

Preface - Message to the Reader

Rebuilding the Greatest Library in Human History

Thousands of years ago, the Library of Alexandria was the heart of global knowledge — a sanctuary where the wisdom of every known civilization was gathered and shared freely.

And then, it was lost.

Now, we're rebuilding it — and you are invited to join us.

At the Library of Alexandria, we've set out to make every book available to *every person on Earth* — not just in print, but in every language, every format, and for every reader.

Here's how we do it:

- **Deluxe Print Editions at True Printing Cost** - Order any book as a high-quality paperback, elegant hardcover, or stunning boxset — and only pay what it costs to print. No markups. No middlemen.
- **Unlimited Access to the Greatest Works** - Enjoy thousands of timeless classics — from Plato to Shakespeare to Tolstoy — in beautiful, modern eBook and audiobook editions. Read and listen without limits — for every reader, everywhere.
- **Modern Translations for Every Language & Dialect** - We're reimagining the classics in clear, accessible language — and translating them into every dialect imaginable. Everyone deserves to understand humanity's greatest ideas.

When you visit **LibraryofAlexandria.com**, you're not just accessing books — you're joining a global movement to restore, preserve, and share the wisdom of civilization.

Join us today at LibraryofAlexandria.com

Together, we'll ensure the light of human wisdom never fades again.

With gratitude,
The Modern Library of Alexandria Team

Visit:
www.libraryofalexandria.com

Or scan the code below:

Prologue

These Oracles are believed to capture many of the key ideas of Chaldean philosophy. They were passed down to us through Greek translations and were highly respected in ancient times, valued by both early Christian leaders and later Platonists. The teachings are attributed to Zoroaster, though which Zoroaster they refer to is unknown, as historians mention up to six different individuals with that name. It is likely that "Zoroaster" was a title for the leader of the Magi, used as a general term. Scholars offer different ideas about the meaning of the name. One of the more interesting interpretations comes from Kircher, who suggests that it could mean "fashioning images of hidden fire" or "the image of secret things," based on a combination of words. Others say the name comes from terms meaning "one who contemplates the stars."

This collection is acknowledged to be fragmented and incomplete, and many of the original meanings have likely been lost or distorted through translation. Where possible, efforts have been made to clarify confusing expressions, either by refining the Greek translation or adding explanatory notes. Some suggest these Oracles were created by the Greeks, but as Stanley points out, Picus de Mirandula claimed to have the original Chaldean text. According to him, the Greek version contained flaws that did not appear in the original, and he stated that he found the manuscript after Mirandula's death. Additionally, some words in the Greek version are not of Greek origin but have Chaldean roots, adapted to the Greek language.

Berosus is believed to have been the first to introduce Chaldean writings on astronomy and philosophy to the Greeks. It is clear that Chaldean traditions had a significant influence on Greek thought. Taylor believed that some of these mystical sayings inspired the philosophical ideas of Plato, and scholars such as Porphyry, Iamblichus, Proclus, Pletho, and Psellus wrote extensive commentaries on them. The fact that such brilliant thinkers held these Oracles in high regard suggests that they deserve our attention.

The name "Oracles" was likely used to emphasize their deep and mysterious nature. The Chaldeans also had an Oracle that they respected as much as the Greeks revered the Oracle at Delphi. Psellus and Pletho both provided detailed commentary on the Chaldean Oracles. Franciscus Patricius later expanded on their work, adding material from other writers, including Proclus, Hermias, Simplicius, Damascius, Synesius, Olympiodorus, Nicephorus, and Arnobius. Patricius compiled around 324 Oracles, organizing them under various topics. His collection, published in Latin in 1593, served as the foundation for later classifications by Taylor and Cory, and their work was used in preparing the current version.

Some of the Oracles collected by Psellus appear to come from an early Chaldean Zoroaster and are marked with the letter "Z," following Taylor's method, with a few exceptions. Another set is attributed to a group of philosophers called Theurgists, who were active during the reign of Marcus Antoninus, as recorded by Proclus. These are marked with the letter "T." Additional Oracles of uncertain origin are labeled "Z or T," while other passages are credited to individual authors where appropriate.

• • •

Introduction

Many people, with good reason, believe that these short and mysterious sayings contain a deep system of mystical philosophy. However, truly understanding this philosophy requires a refined ability to perceive non-physical realities. It is said that the Chaldean Magi passed down their secret knowledge through generations, keeping it alive through tradition from father to son. According to Diodorus, "They do not teach these things as the Greeks do. Among the Chaldeans, philosophy is passed down within families, with sons learning from their fathers. These sons are free from other duties, dedicating themselves fully to learning from their parents, trusting what is taught to them more deeply."

The essence of this oral tradition seems to have survived within these Oracles, which should be studied alongside the teachings of the Kabbalah and Egyptian theology. Those familiar with the Kabbalah know that it can be interpreted in extraordinary ways, especially when paired with the Tarot, which reflects the core ideas of Egyptian theology. If commentators in the past had taken this approach, the Chaldean system within the Oracles would not have been misinterpreted to the extent that it has.

The entire structure of the Hebrew Kabbalah is built on the concept of ten divine powers, each emerging successively from an infinite source of light. These ten powers are seen as the key to understanding all things. They are arranged into three sets of triads, with a tenth power bringing them together. These divine forces extend across four worlds, called Atziluth, Briah, Yetzirah, and Assiah, moving from the most subtle to the most physical. This idea is rooted in pantheism, though it also points toward a divine source. At the heart of all things is the absolute Deity, whose thoughts form the universe we experience.

This same structure applies to the Chaldean system. The diagrams included demonstrate how Chaldean philosophy aligns with the Kabbalah. In the Chaldean view, the "First Mind" and the Intelligible Triad—consisting of Father (Pater), Power (Potentia or Mater), and Mind (Mens)—belong to the realm of higher, non-physical light. The "First Mind" symbolizes the original intelligence that exists within the depths of the divine Father. This intelligence reflects into the "Second Mind," representing divine power in the celestial world. This second mind aligns with the next great triad of divine powers, known as both Intelligible and Intellectual. The third triad belongs to the ethereal world, and it consists of intellectual forces working together.

Finally, the fourth world, known as the Elementary World, is shaped by Hypezokos, or the Flower of Fire, which is the force responsible for building the physical world.

Chaldean theology divided the higher realities into three main levels. The first is Eternal, without a beginning or end, called the "Paternal Depth," the heart of the divine presence. The second is a state of being that has a beginning but no end. This is the Creative World, also known as the Empyrean, which is filled with creations, although its source remains beyond them. The third level is the temporary Ethereal World, which had a beginning in time and will eventually end.

These three worlds are connected by seven spheres. One sphere belongs to the Empyrean, or extends from it, three are part of the Ethereal World, and three exist in the Elementary World, with the physical world uniting them all. These spheres should not be confused with the seven material planets, although the planets represent these spheres physically. The spheres themselves are not material in the usual sense but exist in a deeper, metaphysical way. Psellus tried to link these spheres directly with the planets, but Stanley criticized his approach. However, Stanley's own ideas are not entirely consistent, as he suggests that these worlds are non-physical but also claims that a physical world exists in the Empyrean.

Before the Light of the higher realms, there was the "Paternal Depth," the Absolute Deity that holds all things in potential, always present and unchanging. This idea mirrors the concept of Ain Soph Aur in the Kabbalah—three words, each with three letters, representing three sets of divine powers. These powers become manifest and follow the Triadic Law, guided by the Demiurge, the creator of the universe.

The Light of the higher realms was seen as the first expression of the Paternal Depth, an original and universal essence that flows everywhere and is beyond complete human understanding. The Empyrean is a more refined but still creative fire, serving as the source of the Ethereal World. In turn, the Ethereal World acts as the source for the Elementary World. Through these stages, the ideas of the divine mind become real in time and space.

In many ways, the way of thinking in the East today may not be so different from what it was thousands of years ago. Much that seems strange to us in ancient traditions still resonates with many people around the world. Modern thinkers and scientists have expressed ideas that, while not identical, are similar to these ancient Chaldean beliefs. One example is the idea that natural laws are guided by an intelligent and conscious power. From this point of view, it is not a big leap to see forces as living entities, filling the universe with the creations of the imagination. In this way, history repeats itself, and both ancient and modern ideas reflect the same, ever-changing truth.

Without delving too deeply into metaphysics, it is essential to recognize the importance given to the "Paternal Mind." This is the intelligence of the universe, described poetically as "energizing before energy," which establishes the original patterns of everything that will exist. These patterns are then handed over to the divine powers, known as the Rectores Mundorum, to develop and govern. As the saying goes, "Mind is with Him, power with them."

In the Platonic sense, the word "Intelligible" refers to a way of knowing or perceiving that goes beyond intellectual thought—something higher and distinct from ordinary reasoning. The Chaldeans identified three ways of perceiving: through the senses, through intellectual thought, and through the higher, intelligible concepts. Each of these operates separately, through unique forms or channels. However, their exploration of the soul's nature went much deeper. Though the soul is ultimately connected to the divine, it was seen as a complex being when manifested in existence.

The Oracles speak of the "Paths of the Soul," which are like streams of unyielding fire connecting its essential parts and keeping them whole. These paths, along with its "summits," "fountains," and "vessels," mirror the universal principles that guide everything. This idea, shared by many ancient cosmologies, shows how closely Chaldean metaphysics connect the structure of the universe to the nature of human beings.

In each of the Chaldean Divine Worlds, a group of three divine powers operates together, forming a fourth element that completes the group. As the Oracle says, "In every World, a Triad shines, with the Monad as the ruling principle." These Monads are divine representatives that manage the universe. Each of the four worlds—the Empyrean, Ethereal, Elementary, and Material—is governed by a supreme power that remains directly connected to the Father and guided by divine wisdom. This aligns closely with the Kabbalistic idea of the divine name, which is expressed through four letters in various languages.

The Oracle describes this by saying, "There is a Venerable Name that moves through the Worlds in an unending cycle." The Kabbalah explains this further, teaching that each of the four worlds corresponds to one of the four letters in the divine name. Each world also has its own way of writing this name, reflecting how the order of elements—both on a cosmic and personal level—is governed by the continuous motion of this name. The divine name, associated with the elements, is seen as a universal law that guides creation. This creative force is summed up in the figure known as the Demiurge, or Hypezokos, the "Flower of Fire."

Plato's view of the human being offers a similar idea of the soul's structure. He places intellect in the head, the soul with passions like courage in the heart, and another part of the soul, which contains desires and basic urges, near the stomach and spleen. According to the Chaldean doctrine, as recorded by Psellus, humanity is made up of three types of souls:

First, the Intelligible, or divine soul,

Second, the Intellect or rational soul, and

Third, the Irrational, or passional soul.

This last soul, tied to the body, was thought to change and dissolve at death. The divine soul, according to the Oracles, is described as "a bright fire that, through the Father's power, remains immortal and rules over life." Its influence can only be grasped when the soul moves beyond the illusions created by passions and stops reacting to them.

The rational soul, the Chaldeans taught, can either align itself with the divine or fall under the control of the irrational soul. As the Oracles say, "The divine cannot be reached by those who focus only on the body; only those who strip away these attachments can reach the highest truth." The three types of souls each have their own vehicles. The divine soul's vehicle is immortal, the rational soul's can become immortal through its progress, and the irrational soul is connected to what is called "the image," which is the astral form of the physical body.

Physical life works through these three types of activity. When the body dies, each soul follows a different path, depending on how they used their energies in life. The Oracles encourage people to focus on divine things and resist the urges of the irrational soul, warning, "If you do not succeed, your body will be inhabited by the beasts of the earth."

The Chaldeans assigned the astral form of the irrational soul to the Lunar Sphere. This probably referred to more than just the Moon itself; it included the whole region below the Moon, with Earth at its center. At death, the rational soul rises beyond the Moon's influence, but only if its past life allows for this release. Much importance was placed on how life is lived while the soul is in the body, with frequent calls to seek communion with divine powers. Only the highest form of theurgy was believed to offer such a connection.

"Let the depth of your immortal soul lead you," one Oracle says, "but raise your eyes earnestly upward." Taylor explains this with the idea that "the eyes" represent the soul's inner abilities. When these abilities awaken, the soul becomes filled with a higher life and divine light, almost as if it rises beyond itself.

The Chaldean Magi were said to be the first to separate true visions from dreams. They had a deep understanding of both mental and spiritual realities. Their attention to inner images, along with their passionate devotion, made them more than just teachers—they lived out the philosophy they taught. Life on the open plains of Chaldea, under calm nights and starry skies, nurtured this inner development. From a young age, students of the Magi were taught how to break free from worldly limitations and explore the vast inner realms. One Oracle teaches, "The bonds of the soul, which give her breath, are easy to loosen." Other texts speak of the "Melody of the Ether" and the "Lunar clashings," showing how these mystical experiences reflected real inner practices.

The Oracles also describe how divine visions and impressions appear in the Ether. The Chaldeans believed that the ethers of the elements are the subtle forces through which the more familiar elements—Earth, Air, Water, and Fire—work. These subtle ethers represent the underlying principles of dryness and moisture, heat and cold. The signs of the Zodiac were also linked to these ethers, with each element appearing in three forms. This connection influenced how they understood personality and tendencies. For example, when it was said that someone had Aries rising, it meant that fiery ether dominated their nature, making them energetic and active.

The planets, in turn, were thought to influence the ethers, giving them specific vibrations or energies. These planets, positioned in carefully arranged zones, controlled the flow of these subtle forces throughout the universe.

The Chaldeans believed that the planets were connected not only to specific colors and sounds but also to the ethers, with each planetary force having a special link to certain constellations in the Zodiac. Part of their spiritual practice involved forming connections with these celestial beings. In one fragment, it is said: "If you call upon the celestial Lion often, then, when the heavens disappear from your sight, when the stars lose their light, the moon becomes hidden, and the earth vanishes, you will see everything around you take the shape of a Lion." Both the Chaldeans and Egyptians had a deep understanding of color, which reflected their heightened spiritual awareness. Bright colors were thought to awaken the mind's ability to imagine and engage with inner visions.

The Chaldean method of contemplation involved becoming one with the object of meditation, similar to the process used in Indian Yoga. This approach is captured in the saying, "He becomes one with the images, casting them around himself." Though the divine is without form or body, it was believed that divine forces become temporarily bound to forms for the benefit of humanity.

The subtle ethers served as coverings for the divine Light. The Oracles teach that beyond these ethers lies "a solar world and endless Light." This divine Light was the object of their deepest reverence. However, the Light they sought was not the light of the sun we know. Instead, it was referred to as "the starless sphere above," where "the more true Sun" resides. Theosophists understand this as the idea that the physical sun is just a reflection of a higher, more glorious light.

Some individuals, through their strength, could reach this Light on their own. As the Oracles say, "The mortal who approaches the fire will receive Light from the divine, and the immortal ones are swift to aid those who persevere." However, even those less capable were not entirely left out. The Oracles explain, "Some are blessed with knowledge even as they sleep, drawing strength from the divine." This idea inspired many later thinkers, including Porphyry and Synesius. Apuleius's *Metamorphoses* and the *Vision of Scipio* also reflect this belief. Though many Christians are familiar with the saying "He gives to His beloved in sleep," few fully grasp the deeper meaning behind it.

What, then, was the Chaldean view of earthly life? Were they pessimistic, dismissing the material world as unimportant? It seems more accurate to say that their philosophy was filled with spiritual hope. They believed that beyond the limits of matter lay a better and truer reality. Earthly life was seen as a flawed reflection of this higher realm. Like us, the Chaldeans sought what is good, beautiful, and true. But unlike those who chase external pleasures, they understood that true fulfillment is found within.

The first step in this journey toward inner fulfillment was living a simple life. For most of the Magi, this way of life was ingrained from birth. The discipline of living simply, combined with wisdom, made them especially open to nature's truths. As one Oracle warns: "Do not descend into the dark, glittering world below. Beneath the earth lies a steep fall, where a throne of destructive power awaits. Do not go down into that deceptive splendor, for it will only defile your inner light. Its brilliance is false, and it is home only to the children of sorrow." This beautifully expresses the idea that pursuing physical pleasures diminishes the soul's higher energy. Yet, for those who live virtuously and purify themselves, the Oracles offer encouragement: "The higher powers build up the bodies of the holy ones."

The law of karma was just as important in Chaldean thought as it is in modern theosophy. Ficinus explains, "The soul moves continuously, passing through everything in its journey. Once this journey is complete, it must return through the same paths, weaving a new cycle of life, as Zoroaster teaches: whenever the same causes arise, the same effects will follow."

This is the deeper meaning behind the saying "History repeats itself," far removed from superstitious ideas of fate. Here, everyone receives what they deserve based on their actions, whether good or bad. These are the bonds of life. Yet, the Oracles warn, "Do not expand your destiny," urging people to explore the "River of the Soul." Though the soul serves the body, it can still rise back to the divine order from which it came by combining sacred actions with reason.

We are encouraged to understand the Intelligible, that divine part of being which lies beyond the mind. This can only be grasped with the highest potential of our intellect. The Oracles say, "Understand the Intelligible with the bright flame of an awakened mind." Zoroaster is also credited with saying, "The one who knows himself knows everything within himself." Another teaching suggests that "The Paternal Mind has planted symbols within the soul." However, such knowledge was only available to Theurgists, who, as the Oracles explain, "do not fall into the same fate as the masses." The divine light cannot shine in a disordered soul, just as clouds block the sun. Those who seek higher wisdom without preparation or purity walk a path filled with confusion and darkness, and their efforts will fail.

Even though our destiny may be "written in the stars," the divine soul's mission is to raise the human soul above the circle of necessity. The Oracles praise the power of a will that triumphs over obstacles, describing it like this:

"Hewing down walls with the force of magic, Breaking apart the barriers, Splitting the seven posts to pieces, Speaking the words of mastery!"

This triumph comes through strengthening the will and elevating the imagination, which has the power to guide consciousness. As the Oracles say, "Believe yourself to be beyond the body, and you will be." They might have added, "Then your purified imagination will reveal the symbols of the soul." Yet, when looking within, one must confront the self honestly. "On beholding yourself, fear," meaning you must face the imperfect parts of yourself.

To achieve the highest perfection, everything must be viewed as ideal. Willpower is the key to mystical progress, having a powerful influence over the body's nervous system. Through will, fleeting visions can be held steady within the astral light. Will also drives consciousness toward communion with the divine. However, the challenge lies in aligning three distinct wills—the wills of the Divine Soul, the Rational Soul, and the Irrational Soul.

Selfishness blocks the flow of higher thought, keeping it tied to the body. This is not just a moral idea but a scientific truth. Selfishness beyond basic needs is nothing more than vulgarity. Just as a picture that seems beautiful to a refined mind might look like a mess of colors to someone untrained, so too the broad perspective of one who sees beyond personal concerns cannot be understood by those focused only on themselves.

The path to the greatest good lies through self-sacrifice—offering up the lower self to serve the higher self. Behind this higher self is the hidden presence of the "Ancient of Days," the unified essence of divine humanity. These truths are grasped only by the soul. The soul's song can only be heard in the sacred silence where the divine dwells.

• • •

The Oracles of Zoroaster

CAUSE. GOD.

FATHER.   MIND.   FIRE.
MONAD.   DYAD.   TRIAD.

God is described as having the head of a hawk. He is the first and eternal being, beyond corruption, not created by anything else, whole and unchanging, unlike anything else. He gives all good things, cannot be destroyed, and is the highest good and the wisest. He is the source of fairness, justice, and wisdom, teaching Himself and embodying perfection. He is the inspiration for Sacred Philosophy. Eusebius, *Præparatio Evangelica*, Book 1, Chapter 10. This Oracle isn't found in ancient collections or in the writings of medieval occultists. Cory seems to have found it in Eusebius's writings, where the Persian Zoroaster is credited as its author.

Theurgists say that this God is both old and young. They describe Him as a God who moves endlessly, whose power fills the universe, and who controls everything that moves. He has limitless energy and exerts a force that spirals throughout creation. Proclus on Plato's *Timaeus*, 244. Z. or T. p. 24 In Egyptian mythology, there were two Horuses—an older and younger God—both sons of Osiris and Isis. Taylor suggests that this passage refers to Kronos, or Time, called Chronos by later Platonists. In Roman mythology, Kronos (also called Saturnus) was the son of Uranus and Gaia, married to Rhea, and father of Zeus.

The God of the Universe is eternal and boundless, both young and old, with a spiraling force. Cory includes this Oracle in his collection but doesn't mention its source. Lobeck questioned its authenticity.

The Eternal Æon, according to the Oracle, is the reason for endless life, boundless strength, and tireless energy. Taylor.—T.

The divine ones call this unknowable God "silent" and say He communicates through the power of the Mind. Human souls can only understand Him using their minds. Proclus in *Theology of Plato*, 321. T. The word "inscrutable" is used, though Taylor translates it as "stable," and some suggest "incomprehensible" might be a better term.

The Chaldeans call this God Dionysos (or Bacchus) and Iao in the Phoenician language, referring to Him as the "Intelligible Light." He is also called Sabaoth, meaning He is above the Seven Spheres and acts as the Demiurge. Lydus, *De Mensibus*, 83. T.

He holds all things within Himself, at the peak of His existence, yet He also exists beyond everything. Proclus in *Theology of Plato*, 212. T. "Hyparxis" usually refers to "existence" or "subsistence." "Hupar" suggests reality as distinct from appearance, and "Huparche" means "beginning."

He measures and defines all things. Proclus in *Theology of Plato*, 386. T. The phrase "Thus he speaks the words" appears in the Greek text but is omitted by Taylor and Cory.

Nothing imperfect comes from the Paternal Principle. Psellus, 38; Pletho. Z. This suggests that imperfection only appears through later processes of creation.

The Father did not bring forth fear; instead, He gave the gift of persuasion. Pletho. Z.

The Father fully understands Himself and doesn't limit His fire to His intellectual power alone. Psellus, 30; Pletho, 33. Z. p. 26 Taylor interprets this as "The Father withdrew Himself quickly but didn't confine

His fire to His mind." However, the Greek text doesn't mention "quickly." The word "Arpazo" can mean "grasp" or "understand with the mind."

This is the kind of Mind that exists before action begins, staying in the Father's depth and nourishing silence in the hidden place of God. Proclus on *Timaeus*, 167. T.

Everything comes from the same divine fire. The Father created everything perfectly and passed it to the Second Mind, whom all nations refer to as the First. Psellus, 24; Pletho, 30. Z.

The Second Mind governs the Empyrean World. Damascius, *On Principles*. T.

The Intelligible speaks by understanding. Psellus, 35. Z.

- Power belongs to them, but the source of Mind is from Him. Proclus in *Plato's Theology*, 365. T.
- The Fathers Mind rides upon delicate Guides, which shine with the trails of unwavering and unstoppable Fire. Proclus on Platos *Cratylus*. T.
- After the Fathers thought, I, the Soul, take my place, a warmth that gives life to all things. For He placed The Intelligible within the Soul, and

the Soul within the lifeless body, Just as the Father of Gods and Men has placed these within us. Proclus in *Timaeus*, 124. Z. or T.

- Natures works exist together with the Fathers light of understanding. The Soul decorated the vast Heaven, and after the Father, it continues to shape it. But her rule remains high above. Proclus in *Timaeus*, 106. Z. or T. The word "dominion" is from the Greek *krata*, though some versions use *kerata*, meaning "horns."

- The Soul, as a shining Fire through the Fathers power, remains immortal, ruling over Life and filling the deep places of the Worlds heart. Psellus, 28; Pletho, 11. Z.

- With the channels intertwined, the Soul carries out the works of eternal Fire. Proclus in *Politico*, p. 399. Z. or T.

- The Fire from beyond does not lock its power in matter but exists within the Mind. For it is the Mind of Mind that shapes the Fiery World. Proclus in *Theology*, 333, and *Timaeus*, 157. T.

- The one who first came from Mind wraps one Fire within another, weaving them together to unite the flowing fountains of Fire while keeping its brilliance untouched. Proclus in *Parmenides*. T.

- A Fiery Whirlwind draws down the glow of flashing flames, penetrating the Universes depths, as its marvelous rays extend downwards from there. Proclus in *Plato's Theology*, 171 and 172. T.

- The Monad came first into existence and still remains as the Paternal Monad. Proclus in *Euclid*, 27. T.

- When the Monad stretches outward, the Dyad is born. Proclus in *Euclid*, 27. T. The Pythagoreans describe the Monad, Dyad, and Triad just as Plato does with Bound, Infinite, and Mixed. These Oracles use the terms Hyparxis, Power, and Energy for the same ideas. Damascius *On Principles*. Taylor.

- Beside Him sits the Dyad, sparkling with intellectual divisions. It governs all things and brings order to whatever lacks it. Proclus in *Plato's Theology*, 376. T.

- The Fathers Mind declared that all things should be divided into Three, and with His Wills agreement, everything was immediately separated this way. Proclus in *Parmenides*. T.

- The Eternal Fathers Mind spoke of the Three, ruling everything through understanding. Proclus in *Timaeus*. T.

- The Father blended every Spirit from within this Triad. Lydus, *De Mensibus*, 20. Taylor.

- Everything flows from the heart of this Triad. Lydus, *De Mensibus*, 20. Taylor.

Everything is ruled by and exists within this Triad. Proclus in *First Alcibiades*. T.

You must understand that everything bows before the Three Supreme Powers. Damascius, *On Principles*. T.

From this source comes the Form of the Triad, which existed before creation. It is not the first Essence but the principle by which all things are measured. Anon. Z. or T.

In it appeared Virtue, Wisdom, and all-knowing Truth. Anon. Z. or T.

In every World, the Triad shines brightly, and above it all, the Monad reigns supreme. Damascius in *Parmenides*. T.

The first course is Sacred. In the middle course, the Sun moves, and in the third, the Earth is warmed by inner fire. Anon. Z. or T.

It stands high above, giving life to Light, Fire, Ether, and Worlds. Simplicius in his *Physics*, 143. Z. or T.

Ideas

INTELLIGIBLES, INTELLECTUALS, IYNGES, SYNOCHES, TELETARCHÆ, FOUNTAINS, PRINCIPLES, HECATE AND DÆMONS.

39. The Mind of the Father spun forth with a roaring sound, grasping with unshakable Will every possible Idea. These Ideas, which flowed from a single source, were released, for both the Will and the Purpose came from the Father, and through changing forms of life, they remain connected to Him. But these Ideas were separated and spread by Intellectual Fire into other forms of Intelligence. Before the diverse World took shape, the King of All placed an intellectual and unchanging Pattern as a model. The impression of this Pattern spread throughout the World, filling the Universe with many kinds of Ideas, yet all these Ideas share a single origin. From this

one foundation, they split and spread across different bodies throughout the Universe, moving endlessly through the depths, shining and radiating outward without end. These are intellectual concepts from the Father's Fountain, filled with the brightness of Fire, carried by the flow of unceasing Time. The Father's original, perfect Fountain released these first-born Ideas. Proclus in *Parmenidem*. Z. or T.

40. These Ideas, though many, flash down onto the shining Worlds, carrying with them the Three Divine Powers. Damascius in *Parmenidem*. T.

41. They guard the works of the Father and the One Mind, which holds all understanding. Proclus in *Theologiam Platonis*, 205. T.

42. All things exist together within the World of Pure Intelligence. Damascius, *De Principiis*. T.

43. Every form of Intelligence knows the Divine, for Intelligence cannot exist without the object of its understanding, and the object of understanding cannot exist apart from Intelligence. Damascius. Z. or T.

44. Intelligence depends on what it understands, and without this connection, it cannot exist. Proclus, *Th. Pl.*, 172. Z. or T.

45. Through Intelligence, He holds together the things that can be understood and brings the Soul into the Worlds.

46. With Intelligence, He gathers what can be known and brings Sensation into the Worlds. Proclus in *Crat.* T.

47. The Father's Intelligence, which knows all things and beautifies what cannot be expressed, has scattered symbols throughout the World. Proclus in *Cratylum*. T.

48. This structure is the starting point of all division. Damascius, *De Principiis*. T.

49. Pure Understanding is the root of every division. Damascius, *De Principiis*. T.

50. Pure Understanding serves as nourishment for what gains knowledge. Damascius, *De Principiis*. T.

51. The oracles describe the Order as existing before the Heavens, beyond words, and say it possesses Mystic Silence. Proclus in *Cratylum*. T.

52. The oracle explains that causes born from Understanding are swift. It says that after flowing from the Father, they quickly return to Him again. Proclus in *Cratylum*. T.

53. These Natures are both Intelligent and objects of Intelligence. They hold knowledge within themselves and become subjects for others to understand. Proclus, *Theologiam Platonis*. T. *The Second Order of Platonic philosophy is called the "Intelligible and Intellectual Triad." In Chaldean teachings, this order includes the Iynges, Synoches, and Teletarchs. The later Platonists' Intellectual Triad corresponds with the Chaldean Fountains, Fontal Fathers, or Cosmagogi.*

54. *The Iynges gain their understanding from the Father. Through mysterious guidance, they are moved to comprehend. Psellus, 41; Pletho, 31. Z.*

55. *It is the Operator and the Giver of Life-bearing Fire. It fills Hecate's life-giving womb and transfers the empowering energy of Fire to the Synoches, endowing them with immense strength. Proclus in Timaeus, 128. T.*

56. *He gave His Whirlwinds to guard the Supernals, blending His own force within the Synoches. Dam., On Principles. T.*

57. *Likewise, many others serve the material Synoches. T.*

58. *The Teletarchs are part of the Synoches. Dam., On Principles. T.*

59. *Rhea, the source and river of blessed intellects, holds the powers of all things in her sacred womb, pouring out continuous creation upon everything. Proclus in Cratylus. T.*

60. *She marks the boundary of the Father's Depth and serves as the source of intellect. Dam., On Principles. T.*

61. *He shines with clear, radiant strength, filled with intellectual energy. Dam. T.*

62. *His brilliance contains intellectual power, spreading love throughout everything. Dam. T.*

63. *All things submit to the swirling motions of the Intellectual Fire, following the Father's wise guidance. Proclus in Parmenides. T.*

64. *Oh, how the World is governed by unyielding Intellectual Rulers.*

65. *Hecate's source aligns with that of the Fontal Fathers. T.*

66. *From Him leap forth the Amilicti, unrelenting thunderbolts, and the whirlwinds that fill Hecate's sacred womb with unstoppable strength. He surrounds the brilliance of Fire, and His mighty Spirit, burning beyond, rules the Poles. Proclus in Cratylus. T.*

67. *There is another source that leads the Empyrean World. Proclus in Timaeus. Z. or T.*

68. *It is the source of all sources and the boundary of every spring. Dam., On Principles.*

69. *The fountain that generates life for Souls is contained within two Minds. Dam., On Principles. T.*

70. *Beneath these exists the Primary One of all non-material things. Dam. in Parmenides. Z. or T.*
    Following the Intellectual Triad is the Demiurgos, from whom came the Essences and Orders, including various spirits and the material world.

71. *Light born from the Father alone holds the power to grasp His Mind. It pours understanding into all sources and principles, driving their endless cycles. Proclus in Timaeus, 242.*

72. *All sources and principles revolve continuously, never ceasing their motion. Proclus in Parmenides. Z. or T.*

73. *The principles that have understood the Father's plans are wrapped in physical forms and bodies. These serve as links between the Father and matter, making invisible ideas visible in the world. Dam., On Principles. Z. or T.*

74. *Typhon, Echidna, and Python, children of Tartarus and Gaia, joined by Uranus, form a Chaldean Triad that watches over and controls chaotic creations. Olymp. in Phaedrus. T.*

75. *Some irrational demons, without thought, are sustained by the rulers of the air. This is why the oracle says, "They guide the airy, earthly, and water-dwelling creatures." Olymp. in Phaedrus. T.*

76. *When connected to divine beings, the word "Aquatic" signifies rule tied to water. This is why the oracle calls the aquatic gods "Water Walkers." Proclus in Timaeus, 270. T.*

77. *Some water spirits, known as Nereids in Orpheus's writings, dwell in high, misty waters, appearing in the damp air. As Zoroaster taught, these spirits can sometimes be seen by those with keen sight, especially in Persia and Africa. Ficino, On the Immortality of the Soul, 123. T.*

• • •

Particular Souls

SOUL, LIFE, MAN.

78. The Father created ideas, and He gave life to all mortal bodies. Proclus in *Tim.*, 336. T.

79. The Father of gods and humans placed the Mind (nous) in the Soul (psyche) and placed both within the human body.

80. The Father's Mind planted symbols within the Soul. Psellus, 26; Pletho, 6. Z.

81. He mixed the Vital Spark from two substances—Mind and Divine Spirit—and as a third element, He added Holy Love, the sacred Charioteer that unites all things. Lydus, *De Mensibus*, 3.

82. This Love fills the Soul with deep affection. Proclus in *Platonis Theologia*, 4. Z. or T.

83. The human Soul embraces God closely. It holds no mortal nature and is entirely filled

with God's presence, rejoicing in the harmony that sustains the mortal body. Psellus, 17; Pletho, 10. Z.

84. Stronger Souls can see Truth by their own nature and are more creative. According to the Oracle, such Souls are saved by their own power. Proclus in *I. Alcibiades*. Z.

85. The Oracle says that ascending Souls sing hymns of praise. Olympiodorus in *Phaedrus*. Z. or T.

86. Of all Souls, the most blessed are those sent from Heaven to Earth. They are joyful and possess indescribable strength, for they come from your radiant essence, O King, or from Jove himself, driven by the unbreakable power of Mithus. Synesius, *De Insomniis*, 153. Z. or T.

87. The Souls of those who die suddenly are the purest. Psellus, 27. Z.

88. The threads that hold the Soul's breath can be easily released. Psellus, 32; Pletho, 8. Z.

89. When one Soul is set free, the Father sends another to keep the number complete. Z. or T.

90. By understanding the Father's works, these Souls escape the grasp of Fate. They remain in God's presence, drawing strong lights that descend from the Father. As they descend,

the Soul gathers the heavenly fruit, the flower that nourishes the spirit. Proclus in *Tim.*, 321. Z. or T.

91. This spiritual force, which the blessed call the Pneumatic Soul, becomes a god, a powerful spirit, or an image without a body. In this form, the Soul experiences punishment. The Oracles say that the Soul's tasks in Hades resemble the deceptive visions of a dream. Synesius, *De Insomniis*. Z. or T. The term "Dæmon" originally referred to both good and bad spirits, often applied to pure beings as much as to impure ones. This concept aligns with the Eastern teaching of Devachan, a state of pleasant illusion after death.

92. Life flows from many sources, moving from above, through the opposite side, to the center of the Earth. From there, it reaches the fiery middle point, where the life-giving fire descends into the physical world. Z. or T.

93. Water represents life, which is why Plato and the ancient gods described the Soul as both the water that gives life and the fountain from which it flows. Proclus in *Tim.*, 318. Z.

94. O Man, daring by nature, you are a subtle creation. Psellus, 12; Pletho, 21. Z.

95. Your body will become the home of the beasts of the Earth. Psellus, 36; Pletho, 7. Z. The body is the vessel that temporarily holds the Mind (nous).

96. The Soul moves continuously through different experiences over time. Once these experiences are complete, it must pass through everything again, weaving the same pattern of life in the world. Zoroaster believed that when the same causes arise, the same effects will inevitably follow. Ficinus, *De Immortalitate Animæ*, 129. Z.

97. According to Zoroaster, the Soul's ethereal form continually returns through reincarnation. Ficinus, *De Immortalitate Animæ*, 131. Z.

98. The Oracles celebrate the essential source of every Soul, which flows from the Empyrean, the Ethereal, and the Material realms. They separate this source from Zoogonothea, the life-giving goddess Rhea. From her, they create two orders: one related to the Soul and the other to Fate. The Oracles teach that the Soul comes from the animating order but sometimes falls under the control of Fate. When this happens, the Soul enters an irrational state and becomes subject to Fate

instead of Divine Providence. Proclus, *De Providentia* apud Fabricium, *Bibliotheca Graeca*, vol. 8, 486. Z. or T.

• • •

Matter

THE WORLD--AND NATURE.

99. The Matrix contains everything within it.
T.

100. It can be divided entirely, yet it also remains whole.

101. From it flows the endless creation of many different types of Matter.
Proclus in *Tim.*, 118. T.

102. These creations form atoms, physical shapes, material bodies, and everything that belongs to the realm of matter.
Damascius, *De Principiis*. T.

103. The Nymphs of the Fountains, along with all Water Spirits and forms of the Earth, sky, and stars, are the Riders and Rulers of Matter—whether celestial, starry, or deep within the Abyss.
Lydus, p. 32.

104. The Oracles teach that Evil is weaker than even nothingness.
Proclus, *De Providentia*. Z. or T.

105. Matter fills the whole world, as the gods also proclaim.
Proclus, *Tim.*, 142. Z. or T.

106. Although Divine Beings have no bodies, they are bound to bodies for our sake. Since bodies cannot fully hold spiritual beings due to the limits of material nature, this connection exists to focus the divine within us.
Proclus in *Platonis Politicus*, 359. Z. or T.

107. The Father's Mind, understanding His creations, spread the fiery bonds of love throughout everything, ensuring that all things would remain connected in love for eternity. This way, everything in creation stays linked to the Father's Light, and the elements of the world are drawn together by mutual attraction.
Proclus in *Tim.*, 155. T.

108. The Maker of everything, acting through His own power, shaped the World. Out of a fiery mass, He formed all things by His will, making the Universe a visible creation, not hidden or shapeless.
Proclus in *Tim.*, 154. Z. or T.

109. He made all things in His own likeness, casting them in the image of His form.

110. They reflect His Mind, but because they are made, they also contain something physical.
Proclus in *Tim.*, 87. Z. or T.

111. There is a Holy Name that moves without rest, leaping into the worlds through the Father's rapid vibrations.
Proclus in *Cratylus*. Z. or T.

112. The ethers of the elements are present there.
Olympiodorus in *Phaedrus*. Z. or T.

113. The Oracles reveal that divine symbols and other visions appear within the Ether or Astral Light.
Simplicius in *Physica*, 144. Z. or T.

114. In this realm, the shapeless takes form.
Simplicius in *Physica*, 143. Z. or T.

115. These are the hidden and revealed impressions of the World.

116. The World that resists the Light draws many down through twisting currents.
Proclus in *Tim.*, 339. Z. or T.

117. He made the whole world from Fire, Air, Water, Earth, and nourishing Ether.
Z. or T.

118. He placed the Earth in the center, Water beneath it, and Air above both.
Z. or T.

119. He fixed countless stars in place, keeping them steady and unmoving, with no labor but by stable order, forcing Fire into Fire.
Proclus in *Tim.*, 280. Z. or T.

120. The Father gathered the seven layers of the Cosmos, shaping the Heavens in a curved form.
Damascius in *Parmenides*. Z. or T.

121. He created the seven wandering bodies (the planets).
Z. or T.

122. Their movements were set within well-organized zones.
Z. or T.

123. He made six of them, placing the Fiery Sun as the seventh in the center.
Proclus in *Tim.*, 280. Z. or T.

124. From the center, all lines extend equally in every direction.
Proclus in *Euclidem.*

125. The Sun moves continuously around this central point.
Proclus in *Platonis Theologia*, 317. Z. or T.

126. It eagerly races toward the center of brilliant Light.
Proclus in *Tim.*, 236. T.

127. The Great Sun and the Shining Moon.

128. Its rays spread outward like flowing hair, ending in sharp points.
Proclus in *Platonis Politicus*, 387. T.

129. The movements of the Sun and Moon, the silent spaces of the sky, and the music of Ether join together with the phases of the Sun, Moon, and Air.
Proclus in *Tim.*, 257. Z. or T.

130. The most mysterious teachings say that His completeness is found in the realms beyond this world, where a Solar World and endless Light exist, as the Chaldean Oracles proclaim.
Proclus in *Tim.*, 264. Z. or T.

131. The Sun is the truest measure of time, for it is itself the time of all time, as the Oracle of the gods teaches.
Proclus in *Tim.*, 249. Z. or T.

132. The Sun's disk moves through the starless region above the unchanging sphere and is not among the planets but within the three worlds, according to mystical teachings.
Julian, *Cratylus*, 5, 334. Z. or T.

133. The Sun is Fire, a channel of Fire, and a distributor of Fire.
Proclus in *Tim.*, 141. Z. or T.

134. Thus, Kronos, through the Sun, observes the true pole.

135. The movements of Ether, the Moon's great path, and the changing flows of Air.
Proclus in *Tim.*, 257. Z. or T.

136. O Ether, Sun, and Spirit of the Moon, you are the rulers of the Air.
Proclus in *Tim.*, 257. Z. or T.

137. The wide sky, the Moon's path, and the Sun's pole.
Proclus in *Tim.*, 257. Z. or T.

138. The Goddess brings forth the mighty Sun and the bright Moon.

139. She gathers their light, absorbing the music of Ether, the Sun, the Moon, and all that exists in the Air.

140. Tireless Nature governs the worlds and their motions, ensuring that the Heavens move in an eternal cycle, so the rhythms of the Sun, Moon, seasons, day, and night are fulfilled.
Proclus in *Tim.*, 4, 323. Z. or T.

141. And above the shoulders of the Great Goddess, vast Nature is exalted.
Proclus in *Tim.*, 4. T.

142. The greatest thinkers of Babylon, along with Ostanes and Zoroaster, rightly call the starry spheres "Herds"—either because they alone move perfectly around a center or because, as the Oracles suggest, they gather the principles of nature, which are also called "Herds" (agelous). Adding a "gamma" makes them "Angels" (aggelous). This is why the stars that govern these herds are viewed as divine beings or spirits like Angels and are called Archangels, numbering seven.
Anonymous in *Theologumenis Arithmeticis*. Z.

143. Zoroaster describes the alignment between physical forms and the Soul's ideals as "Divine Allurements."
Ficinus, *De Vita Cælitus Comparanda*. Z.

• • •

Magical And Philosophical Precepts

144. Do not focus your mind on the vast lands of the Earth, for the Plant of Truth does not grow from the ground. Do not try to measure the Sun's movements by creating rules, for it moves by the Father's Eternal Will, not just for your benefit. Let go of the Moon's restless path, for it always moves by the force of necessity. The Stars were not created just for you. The flight of birds through the sky reveals no truth, nor does the examination of animal sacrifices—these are mere illusions, tricks used for profit. Stay away from these if you wish to enter the sacred paradise of devotion, where Virtue, Wisdom, and Justice meet.
Psellus, 4. Z.

145. Do not lower yourself to the shadowy, splendid World, where there lies a deceptive

Depth and Hades, wrapped in clouds, filled with unintelligible images. This dark abyss is treacherous and endlessly churning, always joined with a lifeless and formless body.
Synesius, *De Insomniis*, 140. Z. or T.

146. Do not descend, for beneath the Earth lies a cliff, reached by a ladder with seven steps, and on that path rests the Throne of a destructive and fateful force.
Psellus, 6; Pletho, 2. Z.

147. Do not linger at the edge of the cliff, trapped in material filth, for your true form belongs to a radiant realm.
Psellus, 1, 2; Pletho, 14; Synesius, 140. Z.

148. Do not call upon the visible form of Nature's Soul.
Psellus, 15; Pletho, 23. Z.

149. Do not seek Nature, for her name brings ruin.
Proclus in *Platonis Theologia*, 143. Z.

150. You should not look upon them before your body is initiated, for their allure draws souls away from the sacred mysteries.
Proclus in *I. Alcibiades*. Z. or T.

151. Do not bring her forth, or she may take something with her when she leaves.
Psellus, 3; Pletho, 15. Z.

(Taylor says that "her" refers to the human soul.)

152. Do not corrupt the Spirit or delve too deeply into superficial matters.
Psellus, 19; Pletho, 13. Z.

153. Do not seek to expand your destiny.
Psellus, 37; Pletho, 4.

154. The Oracle says not to step beyond what is required for devotion.
Damascius, *Vita Isidori*. Z. or T.

155. Do not change the sacred names used in invocations, for in every language, God has provided sacred names with great power.
Psellus, 7; Nicephorus. Z. or T.

156. Do not go out when the official passes by.
Picus de Mirandola, *Conclusions*. Z.

157. Let fiery hope sustain you on the angelic plane.
Olympiodorus in *Phaedrus*; Proclus in *Alcibiades*. Z. or T.

158. The glowing Fire comes first, and those who approach it will receive Light from God. The blessed Immortals respond swiftly to those who persevere.
Proclus in *Tim.*, 65. Z. or T.

159. The gods urge us to understand the radiating form of Light.

Proclus in *Cratylus*. Z. or T.

160. You must hasten toward the Light and the Rays of the Father, who sent you a Soul (Psyche) endowed with deep Mind (Nous).
Psellus, 33; Pletho, 6. Z.

161. Seek the path to Paradise.
Psellus, 41; Pletho, 27. Z.

162. Learn what is beyond Mind, for it exists beyond understanding.
Psellus, 41; Pletho, 27. Z.

163. There is one Intelligible Being whom you must grasp with the finest part of your Mind.
Psellus, 31; Pletho, 28. Z.

164. The Paternal Mind will not accept the soul's longing until it awakens from forgetfulness and remembers the sacred symbol of the Father.
Psellus, 39; Pletho, 5. Z.

165. Some are given the ability to know the Light, while others, even in sleep, are blessed with insight from the Father's strength.
Synesius, *De Insomniis*, 135. Z. or T.

166. You must approach the Intelligible Being not with force but with a calm, searching mind, measuring all things except this Being. If you incline your Mind gently, you will understand it—not with effort, but with a pure, inquisitive

sense. Stretch your Soul toward this higher understanding, for it lies beyond ordinary thought.
Damascius. T.

167. You cannot grasp it in the same way you understand common things.
Damascius, *De Primis Principiis*. T.

168. Those who understand must know the deep mysteries of the Paternal Mind beyond this world.
Damascius. Z. or T.

169. Divine truths are not accessible to those focused only on the body. They can only be known by those who, stripped of their earthly attachments, reach the highest summit.
Proclus in *Cratylus*. Z. or T.

170. Clothed in the strength of radiant Light, with triple power protecting both Soul and Mind, one must fill the Mind with sacred symbols and focus, not wander along the celestial path without direction.

171. Armed with every kind of strength, he becomes like the Goddess.
Proclus in *Platonis Theologia*, 324. T.

172. Explore the River of the Soul—know where you came from and in what order. Even

though you have served the body, rise again to the place from which you descended by aligning your actions with sacred reason.
Psellus, 5; Pletho, 1. Z.

173. Fiery rays extend in all directions toward the freed Soul.
Psellus, 11; Pletho, 24. Z.

174. Let the infinite depth of your Soul guide you, and raise your eyes upward with purpose.
Psellus, 11; Pletho, 20.

175. As a rational being, you must control your Soul so it avoids earthly misfortune and finds salvation.
Lydus, *De Mensibus*, 2.

176. If you direct your fiery Mind toward devotion, you will preserve the fragile body.
Psellus, 22; Pletho, 16. Z.

177. A life purified by Divine Fire removes every stain and all irrational impulses that cling to the Soul during its earthly existence, as the Oracle teaches us to believe.
Proclus in *Tim.*, 331. Taylor.

178. The Oracles state that purification rituals benefit not only the Soul but also the body, making it fit to receive help and health. These teachings are given by the gods to the most devoted Theurgists.

Julian, *Cratylus*, 334. Z. or T.

179. The Oracle warns us to avoid following the masses blindly.
Proclus in *I. Alcibiades*. Z. or T.

180. He who knows himself knows everything within himself.
Picus, p. 211. Z.

181. The Oracles emphasize that we have the power to choose, rather than being ruled by the natural order. For example, they say, "When you look at yourself, be mindful," and "If you believe you are more than your body, then you are." Furthermore, they teach that "Our personal struggles shape the kind of life we create."
Proclus, *De Providentia*, p. 483. Z. or T.

182. These are deep mysteries I explore in the profound Abyss of the Mind.

183. The Oracle says that God does not abandon us unless we approach divine matters with confusion or impurity. If we do so, our progress is incomplete, our efforts are wasted, and the path becomes dark.
Proclus in *Parmenides*. Z. or T.

184. If you do not recognize that every god is good, you remain vigilant for nothing.
Proclus in *Platonis Politicus*, 355. Z. or T.

185. Theurgists do not fall into the ranks of those controlled by Fate.
Lydus, *De Mensibus*. Taylor.

186. The number nine, composed of three triads, reaches the highest level of theology, as the Chaldean philosophy teaches through Porphyry.
Lydus, p. 121.

187. On Hecate's left side is a fountain of Virtue that remains untouched and pure.
Psellus, 13; Pletho, 9. Z.

188. Even the Earth mourned for them and their children.
Psellus, 21; Pletho, 3. Z.

189. The Furies are the enforcers of punishment upon humans.
Psellus, 26; Pletho, 19. Z.

190. Do not become trapped by the Furies of Earth or the demands of nature, or you will perish.
Proclus in *Theologia*, 297. Z. or T.

191. Nature teaches us that there are pure spirits, and that even the harmful seeds of matter can be transformed into something useful and good.
Psell., 16; Pletho, 18. Z.

192. You only need to offer sacrifices for three days, no more.

Pic. Concl. Z.

193. Before anything else, the priest in charge of the works of fire must sprinkle water from the roaring sea.
Proc. in Crat. Z. or T.

194. Work diligently around the sacred wheel of Hecate.
Psell., 9. Nicephorus.

195. When you see an earthly spirit approaching, shout out loud and offer the stone Mnizourin as a sacrifice.
Psell., 40. Z.

196. If you call upon these forces often, you will notice everything around you fading into darkness. The sky will no longer be visible, the stars will lose their light, and the moon will be hidden. The Earth itself will feel absent, lightning will flash around you, and thunder will fill the air.
Psell., 10; Pletho, 22. Z.

197. From the depths of the Earth will spring forth demons with the faces of dogs, offering no real sign to guide mortals.
Psell., 23; Pletho, 10. Z.

198. A similar fire will rush through the air, formless and chaotic, bringing with it the sound of a voice or a swirling flash of light.

You may see the vision of a fiery horse, or a child riding on a celestial steed—either clothed in gold, naked, or shooting arrows of light while standing on the horse's shoulders. If you focus deeply in meditation, you will be able to unite these visions into the image of a lion.
Proc. in Pl. Polit., 380; Stanley Hist. Philos. Z. or T.

199. When you see the holy, formless fire shining through the depths of the universe, listen closely and hear the voice of the fire.
Psell., 14; Pletho, 25. Z.

• • •

Oracles From Porphyry

1. Above the celestial lights, there is an eternal flame that sparkles without end. It is the source of life and the origin of all beings, the beginning of everything! This flame brings everything into existence, and nothing is destroyed except by its consuming fire. It reveals itself by its own nature. This fire cannot be contained in any place, for it has no physical form and no material substance. It surrounds the heavens entirely. From it, tiny sparks emerge, creating all the fires of the Sun, the Moon, and the Stars. This is what I understand about God. Do not seek to know more, for no matter how wise you are, it is beyond human comprehension. Know this: unjust and wicked people cannot hide from God's presence! No clever trick or excuse can conceal anything from His all-seeing eyes. God is present in everything, and everything is filled with God!

2. Within God is a vast depth of flame! Yet, the heart should not fear approaching this sacred fire or being touched by it. It is a gentle fire that will not destroy you. Its calm and soothing heat binds everything together, bringing harmony and stability to the world. Nothing exists without this fire, for it is God Himself. He has no creator and no mother. He knows all things and cannot be taught anything. His plans are perfect, and His name is beyond words. This is what God is! As for us, His messengers, we are only a small part of God.

...

The End

Thank you for Reading

You've Just Read a Piece of the Greatest Library Ever Rebuilt

Thank you for reading.

This book is one of thousands we're restoring, reimagining, and translating as part of the **Modern Library of Alexandria** — a global movement to preserve and share humanity's most important ideas.

What was once lost to fire and time is now rising again — not just as memory, but as living, breathing knowledge, freely accessible to all.

What You Can Do Next:

- **Keep Reading.**

    Discover more legendary works — in beautiful print, audiobook, or digital form — at LibraryofAlexandria.com.

- **Build Your Own Library.**

    Every title is available as a paperback, hardcover, or collectible boxset — at true printing cost. Craft a personal library worthy of display.

- **Spread the Light.**

    Share this book. Tell others about the movement. Help us translate every timeless work into every language, so no reader is ever left behind.

By finishing this book, you've already taken part in something extraordinary.

Join us at LibraryofAlexandria.com

Together, we're rebuilding the greatest library the world has ever known.

With appreciation,
The Modern Library of Alexandria Team

Visit:

www.libraryofalexandria.com

Or scan the code below:

www.ingramcontent.com/pod-product-compliance
Lightning Source LLC
LaVergne TN
LVHW030631080426
835512LV00021B/3454